WOMEN MOVING
FORWARD®

WOMEN MOVING
FORWARD®

12 Years of the Women's
Leadership Retreat Concepts

SUSAN BASH VAN VLEET

ARCHWAY
PUBLISHING

Archway Publishing books may be ordered through booksellers or by contacting:

Archway Publishing
1663 Liberty Drive
Bloomington, IN 47403
www.archwaypublishing.com
1 (888) 242-5904

Because of the dynamic nature of the Internet, any web addresses or links contained in this book may have changed since publication and may no longer be valid. The views expressed in this work are solely those of the author and do not necessarily reflect the views of the publisher, and the publisher hereby disclaims any responsibility for them.

Any people depicted in stock imagery provided by Thinkstock are models, and such images are being used for illustrative purposes only. Certain stock imagery © Thinkstock.

ISBN: 978-1-4808-2872-8 (sc)
ISBN: 978-1-4808-2873-5 (e)

Library of Congress Control Number: 2016935188

Print information available on the last page.

Archway Publishing rev. date: 8/5/2016

"I received the gift of being referred to WMF early in my career and have benefited from learning and applying the course concepts for the past 20+ years. If you are ready to stop making excuses, understand what you want to accomplish and put a plan in place to overcome what is getting in your way, it is time to roll up your sleeves and sign up for this terrific training. It has the power to change your life as well as the lives of those who you come in contact with...."

Kate Johnson, President
Gracecamp Consulting

We are all able to navigate around and avoid the obvious obstacles in our lives. But what about the things we can't see? Or the things of which we are unaware? Women Moving Forward helped me to understand and appreciate myself by removing barriers that I did not know existed. Susan is one of the most insightful, clear, and self-actualized women I have had the opportunity to meet. Her unique blend of candor and insight helped me to be truly aware of myself, my needs, what really goes on around me or _choices that I make_ that rob me of my power and peace of mind. The result? Freedom. I recommend this program without reservation. Susan is changing the world for the better, one woman at a time.

I continue to grow and change for the better years after Women Moving Forward. Apparently, once the flower is encouraged to bloom, it cannot return to being a "bud".

With love and affection,
Diane

"Women Moving Forward® and the Women's Leadership Retreat© have been life changing for me! I wouldn't have the life I have and love today if it weren't for Susan and these workshops!"

"There are so many situations in my life when I can hear Susan's voice saying, 'There just hopping' or 'You need to get over your feeling of powerlessness'; I immediately get back on the right track."

Robin Elston
President
RElston@ElstonConsulting.com
Elston Consulting, LLC

I am only a very recent graduate of WMF (September '08), but what a fabulous experience. My only wish was that I had done it 20 years ago! A colleague who had been on WMF described it as a "gift from the company", which intrigued me and was the final decider in joining. As a Brit we are not so good at the more "touchy/feely" stuff, so was very nervous about going. However I was truly liberated by the experience of WMF, at last realising that I was the only person stopping me from anything I choose to do. The joy and strength I gained from being with a group of women was fantastic and it has really made me appreciate not only my long standing female friends but also how wonderful it is to make new ones. Susan – thank you, thank you and may there be another 30 years!!

Kind regards
Polly

The Women Moving Forward course and learning sharpens your self awareness and explore to be better person in life!

Phoebe Wang, P&G China

-WMF profoundly and permanently affected my life more than any other class or workshop I've experienced.

-Quite simply, it works. You'll know what to do to get 'unstuck.'

-You can't believe the impact just 3 days will have!

-WMF and Susan VV opened my eyes and changed my life. My work and my personal life are forever impacted by the insights and tools from the workshop.

-After WMF, I have a clearer view of myself, the environment around me and how I react. I'm better equipped to stay focused on what matters, leading to improved productivity & effectiveness in all parts of my life.

-Highly recommended for anyone who wants to live with purpose and awareness.

-Come learn how to live on purpose. Your work and life will be better, and the world needs you on purpose.

Chris Nassivera, P&G Boston

I recall the retreat being quite impactful as I had recently completed rounds of chemotherapy and radiation to treat breast cancer. Going through an experience like that, as you might expect, can be quite traumatic, and I found the Leadership Retreat to be an enabler for getting re-grounded post treatment. In other words, it helped to ease back into more of a "normal" professional and personal circumstance while not losing sight of the important lessons I learned during that time. As you teach "living on purpose" as a key element for achieving personal and professional goals as part of the WLR I was able to see how to refocus much of the emotion/energy spent on my treatment experience into more purposeful vein.

Jill Boughton, President & CEO, Sustainable
Waste Resources International

Speaking on behalf of Robin as well, I can tell you this was probably one of the most powerful and effective trainings we've ever attended. The premise of this specific workshop was to help the individual identify the barriers preventing you from achieving your best possible professional performance and then develop strategies and techniques for breaking down these barriers allowing you to be the best leader you can be. These barriers are both internally created, but also external barriers. This particular workshop is very introspective (almost therapeutic) and to be honest, it drums up as many personal issues and development needs as it does professional issues and development needs. The idea is, we each have varying experiences (both positive and negative) that have influenced who we are, how we handle situations, and how we communicate and interact with colleagues on a daily basis. Often, the negative experiences you may have had in your life create obstacles (unconsciously and often self-imposed) for your continued development. Somehow Susan is able to ask the right questions allowing you to identify these barriers when you may not have ever connected the dots yourself. After getting to that point (by end of Day 2) she then has you work through exercises that creates a cognizance, goals, objectives, further obstacles, and remedies for those obstacles, and she requires you to identify a timeline to address each. By the nature of what is discovered in Days 1 and 2, these generally aren't simple goals you can achieve in a matter of months or even a year, but rather these are bigger, more strategic goals for personal and professional development. I plan to discuss mine with Mark in my next MAPP meeting.

Nicole McGrath, Assistant Comptroller, Steelcase

The combination of having a room full of amazing successful women with such a mixture of experiences and stories to share and a structure to understand how to achieve your purpose in life makes this course terrific.

Sumaira Latif, IT UK

"The Women Moving Forward® course offered by Susan Van Vleet Consultants, Inc. was such a unique experience and journey that really helped me unlock my true self and understand what had been holding me back in my career and my life. This course helped me identify how I can take charge of my whole life and self and live more fully I highly recommend this course for anyone looking to discover their true potential!"

Cynthia Herrera, SCJ Sales

Women Moving Forward is the best thing that happened to me in the area of personal training. It gave me the ability to proactively enhance the relationship with myself (=self confidence) and with my company. This ability makes me a better manager and a better person in life as well.

Linda Bus-Jacobs
PE Manager
Process Excellence & Transformation

"WMF is a life changing experience for women that given some internal and external barriers can't develop themselves to their full potential. WMF has enabled me to be a better mentor and help other women identify some attitudes/beliefs that we not helping them grow and develop to the next level".

Regards,
Claudia Herreramoro
Mexico

WMF changed the entire trajectory of my life. I stopped living the life I thought I was expected to live and started living a life I'd only dreamed was possible.

Hilary Beard
New York Times Best Seller Author

Contents

Introduction

In 2001, I designed and unveiled a special Women's Leadership Retreat® for the graduates of Women Moving Forward®. It was designed to cover all of the topics and exercises we don't have time to do in Women Moving Forward®. Needless to say, it has expanded since then!

For the last twelve years, the Women's Leadership Retreat® has successfully facilitated a discussion amongst top-level women in their respective fields. The discussion, or as I like to call it, **The Conversations,** began in 2001 with a foundation for discovering your purpose in life. Each year, we introduce one to three new concepts. We are currently up to thirty-one concepts.

Every year we return these women to their purposes and their abilities to intend and create results in the world.

This book is a compilation of the first thirty-one concepts and the exercises that we developed to help women integrate the concepts into their repertoires of behaviors.

The Women's Leadership Retreat® is a safe place for women from major multinational corporations to gather and discuss the issues and concepts important to their lives, enabling them to live purposefully and with great satisfaction.

The participants are director level or above and usually come from three to four different countries. They include medical doctors and VPs of companies, as well as company CEOs.

Because we only have space for twelve to fourteen women each year in the Women's Leadership Retreat® we decided to release the twenty-seven concepts in a format that we use in the workshop so women can work through the eleven years of retreat concepts in the comfort of their own home.

Enjoy your own private Women's Leadership Retreat®!

Directions

We recommend that you begin with Concepts #1-5. This will help you with the foundation you will need to work on the later concepts. Discovering your purpose and then having it be the context of your life may take you a while. It is a process, not a first quarter goal. Many of the women who attend the Women's Leadership Retreat® are still in the process of discovering and living out of their purposes.

We have also provided you with a bibliography of books and films we have used with participants during the twelve years. We think you will find them helpful as you begin the process of working through the concepts.

We are, of course, not the first to write about these concepts, nor will we be the last. We have always wanted participants to have access to the books and films created by people who have already tackled those concepts.

After you work through Concepts #1-5, we invite you to then select whichever concept you feel would be important to deal with next. If you want to do them in order, that's fine too.

We look forward to hearing from you after you have read the book and done the exercises.

You can always contact us through our websites:
www.svanvleetconsult.com and www.womenmovingforward.com

Susan

Concept #1
Your Purpose in Life

Concept #1
Purpose in Life

Purpose is the context of your life. It is why you were put on this earth this time.

→ Read 2002 Worksheet #1 – Characteristics / Properties of Purpose

→ Try to write your purpose (2002 Worksheet, Your Purpose in Life). You may revise it many times before you feel it is a fit for you. That's okay. Force yourself to start by writing something and then read it over and over until you want to re-write it. You may have to do this several times before you are satisfied.

Characteristics /
Properties of Purpose

1. You cannot control the format, form or experience of your purpose. It controls you.

2. Purpose is not a goal.

3. Purpose has no prescribed form. You can express it in many forms.

4. You cannot force a purpose on anyone. Everyone must discover his or her own.

5. Your purpose is the context of your life, not the content.

6. Your purpose is larger than you are and will not be accomplished when you die!

Your Purpose in Life

1. **If you know your purpose, please state it here:**

   _____

   _____

   _____

   _____

2. **To get closer to a statement of your purpose, answer the following questions:**

   a. What contributions to society and/or to the world do you want to make before you die?

      _____

      _____

      _____

   b. What do you want said in your eulogy about what you accomplished in life?

      _____

      _____

      _____

Concept #2

Being On Purpose,
Being Off Purpose

Concept #2

Being On Purpose, Being Off Purpose

Sometimes "Life Happens" and you forget to live your life with your purpose as its' context. We say you are "off purpose". Meaning the content of your life is becoming your reason for being.

For example, when my mother died, my grief took me off purpose, which was necessary and normal at the time.

→ Read the Off Purpose / On Purpose Chart

→ Fill out 2002 Worksheet #4, Off Purpose
List as much as possible about what may be in your way in your life to living out of your purpose

→ Fill out 2002 Worksheet #5, On Purpose
List what support you will need in *your* life to live your life on purpose. Don't be afraid or ashamed to list everything you can think of.

SUSAN VAN VLEET CONSULTANTS, INC. ® 2001

Off Purpose, On Purpose Chart

When You Are...

Off Purpose	On Purpose
1. You feel icky / something is wrong and you don't know what / you feel out of sync	1. Everything fits like a puzzle that has come together
2. You constantly feel you must push or pull things to get anything done	2. You do not need to push or pull anything – it flows naturally
3. People "suck you dry" or you have to "dumb down" to be with them. You have little or no support	3. Support comes from everyone and everywhere. Those who don't support you in your purpose go away
4. You are floundering / not making decisions	4. You are taking a stand
5. You force things to happen, you create little	5. You create through intention

SUSAN VAN VLEET CONSULTANTS, INC. ® 2001

Off Purpose

1. What part of your life is in the way?

   a. people
   b. finances
   c. structure
   d. etc.

On Purpose

2. What support do you need to stay on purpose?

    a. people
    b. finances
    c. structure
    d. etc.

Concept #3
Intention and Creation

Concept #3
Intention and Creation

When we say, *"What you intend, you create; what you create, you intend,"* what does it mean to you and why?

Think about that phrase and what it would mean in your life.

Definitions:

Intend: A determination to act in a certain way. Resolve; what one intends to do or be about.

Create: The act of creativity, to bring into existence, to produce or bring about by a course of action or behavior (bring into being).

→ All of this takes place in language – in your assertions and declarations

Declaration: A statement with no basis in fact, no evidence.

SUSAN VAN VLEET CONSULTANTS, INC. ® 2001

Intentions and Creations

1. List all of what you remember you intended over the last five years.

2. List all of what you remember you created over the last five years.

Concept #4
Declarations of Self

Concept #4
Declarations of Self

To shift who you think you are so you can live out of purpose you must first:

- List all of your old declarations of self and declare them complete or over, depending on their status. In other words, give them up.

What you say about yourself defines you - It becomes real because you said it. So you must be more purposeful in your description of yourself.

Review these things you say about yourself yearly, as a lot of the old things you say are probably no longer true for you.

It also helps to complete some of these declarations so you can have the room to make new, more current and helpful declarations.

Declarations about Self

1. List all of the old declarations you have about yourself.

2. Cross out which ones you can declare complete and let go of them.

3. Mark with an asterisk (*) which declarations are still true.

4. Make at least ten new declarations about yourself.

SUSAN VAN VLEET CONSULTANTS, INC.® 2001

Concept #5

Creating Out Of Nothing

Concept #5
Creating Out of Nothing

The act of creating is to bring into existence, to produce or bring about by a course of action or behavior.

The key to creating is that all creation first starts because you say so. It starts by you declaring or asserting something. For example, I will start my business and be profitable in two years. This declaration is necessary to create a business.

To create, you must first intend something. Intending is making a declaration to yourself.

Then you must declare it to the world. Say it openly.

Creating Out of Nothing

What have you created in the last year for yourself or others?

What process did you use to create it?

Looking back, what was your intention (declaration to yourself) that started this process?

SUSAN VAN VLEET CONSULTANTS, INC. ® 2001

Concept #6
Love and Responsibility

Concept #6
Love and Responsibility

Love is a declaration, a statement of what you intend – it has no basis in fact, and there is no evidence for it.

Responsibility for Love

- Women must declare their love repeatedly; it is not just a one-time declaration.

- Always check your declarations about love for the ones you want to discard, recreate or make newly.

- You may have Intentions about love but to make them real – move them from intention to creation - you must make a declaration out loud.

- When you make declarations about love you must be willing to be responsible for them. So don't make them unless you are willing to be responsible for them. For example; when I finally said I wanted to be married and have children in two years, John, my husband, appeared. It can be and seem almost magical when it is really you creating the relationship and love you want.

Love

What are your current declarations about love?

Love

What are your current intentions about love?

Concept #7

Responsibility at the Level of Intention and Creation

Concept #7

Responsibility at the level of intention and creation

Responsibility at the Level of Intention and Creation

- You must own the bad stuff *and* the good stuff, not just the bad stuff.

- You must be willing to own that you created what you have now.

- When you say you want something (you declare it, and it doesn't appear) look and see if you are willing to be responsible for it and for the creation of it.

- You must own that once you get what you created and it's not really what you wanted, it's your creation not someone else's. You can't blame someone else for it's existence.

- You cannot make yourself wrong – there is no place for that in intention and creation. There is only room for the declaration; "I'm going to love myself no matter what". If you always operate from intention and creation, who you have defined yourself as in the past is gone.

Love

With regard to love, what are you willing to create and be responsible for?

Love and Purpose

With regard to Love, how will you live your life out of your purpose?

Concept #8
Self-Love

Concept #8

2005 WLR

Self Love

Self-love is the act of loving yourself as you are, moment to moment. Self-love does not equal assessing yourself.

If you live out of your purpose, some people won't like you.

To love yourself as you are, with no assessment, and live out of purpose, you will need to suspend certain assessments of yourself.

Self Love

The act of loving yourself as you are, moment by moment. Self-love does not equal assessing yourself.

Do you love yourself as you are, moment by moment?

Yes _____

No _____

If no, why not?

What would you have to suspend to love yourself as you are?

Concept #9

Breakdown and Assessment

Concept #9

2005 Worksheet 4C

Breakdown and Assessment

As soon as you make a commitment out of your purpose you choose to put yourself into breakdown.

Breakdown is the state of recognizing the intention you have, seeing all that is in they way of creating it in the world and not accomplishing it yet.

Assessment is the act of judging, determining the rate or amount of, making an official valuation of and determining the importance, size and value of something.

While in **breakdown,** assessment becomes an analytical tool, *do not make it a way of life.*

If you make assessment a way of life, you are no longer in the creation realm. Instead, you are in the judging and assessing realm. How quickly can you move from realm to realm?

Concept #10

*Everything Happens
in Language*

Concept #10

2006 WLR

Dr. Fernando Flores has said everything happens in Language

All of your declarations and assertions define who and what you are, as well as who and what you are not.

Your negative declarations have costs to you.

Ultimately these declarations are you punishing yourself!

Do you really need these declarations?

Do you need to punish yourself?

If you do need to punish yourself, why?

What you say and how you say it matters.

Declarations about Self

1. List all of the old Declarations you have about yourself.

2. Cross-out the ones you can declare complete and can let go of.

3. Mark with an asterisk (*) which declarations are still true.

4. Make at least ten new declarations about yourself.

Negative Declarations of Self

List five of the most negative declarations of self you have.

1.

2.

3.

4.

5.

The Cost of Your Negative Declarations of Self

For each negative declaration you listed on Worksheet #4, list three costs to you of that declaration.

Declaration #1   *COSTS*   1. _____
                               2. _____
                               3. _____

Declaration #2   *COSTS*   1. _____
                               2. _____
                               3. _____

Declaration #3   *COSTS*   1. _____
                               2. _____
                               3. _____

Declaration #4   *COSTS*   1. _____
                               2. _____
                               3. _____

Declaration #5   *COSTS*   1. _____
                               2. _____
                               3. _____

Concept #11
Responsibility

Concept #11

2006 WLR

Responsibility

As we get older, we realize we are totally responsible for all of our negative declarations of self.

No one else is responsible; we are the only ones responsible.

Take responsibility for all of your negative declarations and why you created them. Accept your own imperfections.

Can you commit to leading an imperfect life purposefully?

What if you have already done everything you were supposed to do in life? What if there is nothing more expected of you? How would you need to live your life of this were true?

Concept #12
Purging Old Declarations and Fears

Concept #12

2006 WLR

Purging Old Declarations and Fears

You must regularly purge your old negative declarations.

We recommend some kind of ceremony – in which you burn, shred or tear up your negative declarations.

After you have purged them read QUOTE: Our Deepest Fear by Marianne Williamson

FEAR

It's just an emotion.

It's not more or less important than any other emotion.

You don't need to "conquer" or "get over" your fears, just carry the fear with you as you move forward.

Concept #13
Acknowledgments

Concept #13

Acknowledgments

Acknowledgments are assertions you can make about yourself or others. They can be proven with evidence.

All acknowledgments have two parts:

1. A statement of what the person did / did not do or say

    and

2. A statement of how that manifested / or what that meant to you or others

Most people block or deflect acknowledgement.

It is difficult to accept acknowledgment as it is given with nothing added or deleted.

It takes practice to effectively receive or deliver acknowledgments.

*Question: Can I lead a purposeful life and also acknowledge myself?

Acknowledgments of Self

List five new acknowledgments of yourself. Remember to include:

- What you did/did not do or say
- What that meant to you or others

1.

2.

3.

4.

5.

Acknowledgments of Others

Write a true acknowledgment of ten people you know, including both parts of the acknowledgment.

Now, deliver them until the person "gets it", or until they let them (the acknowledgment) in.

Have another person deliver five acknowledgements to you. They must keep delivering them until you "get it", or let them in.

Concept #14

Internal v. External Validation

Concept #14

Internal v. External Validation

When you live a purposeful life you must know where you get most of your validation from.

Internal Validation is your validation of yourself even when no one else will. You declare yourself valid, you give yourself your official sanction, you substantiate you.

External Validation is the validation you receive from outside of you; from family, friends, co-workers, bosses, institutions, etc.

We all need some external validation, but the more you rely on external validation, the more your wellbeing is dependent on others.

You must be able to rely on your internal compass if you plan to live a purposeful life.

In the parts of your life where you need more external validation it is likely you are looking at a "picture" of how you think it *should* be that you can't fulfill so you need more external validation.

For example, if you have a "picture" of what a successful VP is in your company, how you "should be" to be a VP at your company and you know you can't fulfill that "picture" you need to seek out external validation that you can be a VP or external validation that you can't be a VP.

An alternative is to rid yourself of the picture and move forward by restructuring the VP job for your needs and the company needs.

Definition of Dissonance

Lack of agreement, consistency or harmony; conflict.

Definition of Validation

1. Being declared or made legally valid

2. To mark with an indication of official sanction

3. To substantiate

Internal v. External Validation

% of Internal Validation Needed		% of External Validation Needed and From Whom
Your personal relationships with significant others		
Your personal relationships with kids		
Your work		
Your relationship with a higher power / your spirituality		
Your appearance		
Your successes		
Your failures		

Concept #15

Shifting Domains Takes a Declaration

Concept #15

2008 WLR

Shifting Domains Takes a Declaration

Creating out of nothing takes an action in language. We are constantly shifting from one domain to another domain every moment of every day.

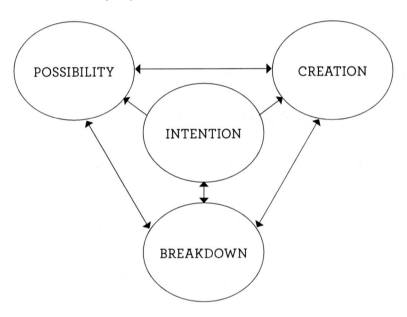

You can't wait for it to "look like" it will happen or "go your way," and if you continually "take what you get," you will always be "putting up with your life".

To shift to living your life by creating out of your intention, you must declare what you intend possible.

The Power of Declaration

Looking back on the last year list three things you intended and created, what declaration did you make that initiated each of the creations?

What you created	The declaration that started the creation

List Three Intentions You Have:

1.

2.

3.

What happens when you list them? Explain.

Concept #16

Relationships with Men

Concept #16

Relationships with Men

Women are never initially in relationships (work or personal) with the man as he really is.

Women are in relationships with their *fantasy* or their *idea* of who the man is, not who the man actually is.

It takes three to seven years of a relationship with a man for a woman to strip away her fantasy or idea of who the man is, and see the him for who he actually is.

Then the woman must begin the *real relationship* with the *real man*. This takes the woman recommitting to the relationship or not.

The State of Your Relationships with Men

The negative declarations you have for the men in your life are really a measure of how you feel about yourself.

For example:

When you are continually surprised at how much men are behind you in something, that means you are *undervaluing* and *underestimating* who you are, n*ot over-estimating* who they are!

Men of Your World/Your Relationships with Them

What declaration do you have to change about you?	List your top five current relationships with men.	List your negative declarations for these men.	What is the relationship cost of your declaration?
1.			
2.			
3.			
4.			
5.			

Concept #17

The Already Listening of Men and Women

Concept #17

2008 WLR

The Already Listening of Men and Women

No one shows up in your space and you don't show up in other people's space without an "already listening", that voice in your head that shows up when you are silent. Be quiet for three minutes and listen to your own voice in your head.

You already have a whole host of ideas, declarations and assertions that show up where and when you show up. That is your "already listening".

Imagine what you are really doing in attempting to speak into the already listening (voice in the head) of the people you are communicating with. When you attempt to do this with men, you must go across the gender divide between your already listening and theirs.

For some of you the gap or divide is smaller than for others (see list on page 50 of *Brain Sex* by Anne Moir, Ph.D. and David Jessell).

Hint: To speak into men's "already listening" you must:

1. Stop devaluing yourself.
2. Know what your voice in your head/already listening is saying and stop listening to it.
3. Start speaking to men where *they are* not where you want them to be or hope they are or will be.

What is the already listening of men?

1. List an incident (unresolved) that you have with a man in your personal life or work life:

2. Determine your already listening:

3. Determine the man's already listening:

4. How could you speak into his already listening?

Concept #18

Presenting Emotion and Underlying Emotions

Concept #18

2009 WLR

Presenting Emotion and Underlying Emotions

If you want to change the nature of your relationships today, then you need to *complete emotions from the past.*

The first step to completing past emotions is to recall them and talk about them, usually with another human being who can listen and get what you are saying.

The second step is to make sure you are recalling and sharing the *underlying emotion* you felt and not the one you are using to hide the underling emotion.

The emotion you use to cover up your true emotion is called the *presenting emotion.*

The *presenting emotion* is the emotion you are not afraid to express. Under that emotion is the *underling emotion* you felt.

The underlying emotions are the one's you're truly afraid to speak of and feel.

- Fill out **Worksheet #1, What Do You Need to Complete?**
- Then fill out **Worksheet #5, Presenting Emotion/Underlying Emotion.**
- Use the emotions listed on **Worksheet #2, Emotions Worksheet** to put words to what you are feeling.

2009 Worksheet #1

What Do You Need to Complete?

What incidents in your life are still incomplete? Pick two and list them below. Make sure you describe each incident fully; Who was there? What was not there? When was it? How old were you? What emotions did you feel, or, do you still feel?

Incident #1:

Emotions you felt and still feel:

What do you think you need to do to complete this for yourself?

2009 Worksheet #1
2009 Women's Leadership Retreat®
What Do You Need to Complete?

Incident #2:

Emotions you felt and still feel:

What do you think you need to do to complete this for yourself?

2009 Women's Leadership Retreat

Presenting Emotion / Underlying Emotion

List the emotion you usually express first:

What emotions are you protecting yourself from expressing by expressing that presenting emotion (listed above)?

1. _____

2. _____

3. _____

4. _____

5. _____

Emotions Worksheet

relieved	realistic	depressed
thrilled	guilty	anxious
sad	loss	oblivious
worried	let people down	somber
resentful	bitter	sullen
angry	disillusioned	serious
hopeful	helpless	hurt
disappointed	used	betrayed
enraged	cynical	cheated
resigned	burned out	shock
tenuous	out of control	disbelief
doubtful	inadequate	excited
apathetic	trapped	frustrated
envious	overwhelmed	vengeful
despondent	abandoned	accepting
relaxed	gleeful	desperate
numb	confused	ashamed
self-indulgent	dazed	failure
disgusted	scared	proud
impotent	silly	suspicious
isolated	embarrassed	

Concept #19
Hate

Concept #19

2009 WLR

Hate

The emotion called hate is an interesting emotion.

Definition: Intense hostility and aversion usually deriving from fear, anger or sense of injury. Extreme dislike or antipathy; loathing.

By definition, you cannot feel hate for someone that you don't feel strongly for.

The opposite of hate is not love, it is antipathy. Antipathy is the absence of feeling for someone.

Most people feel hate when they are hurt by someone they once loved or liked.

Fill out Worksheet #3, **Who Do You Hate?**

2009 Women's Leadership Retreat®

Hate

Who do you hate?

Why?

Concept #20
Anger, a "Glop" Emotion

Concept #20

2009 WLR

Anger, A "Glop" Emotion

Anger: A strong feeling of displeasure and usually antagonism from the Latin; Angare = to strangle.

Anger is what we refer to as a *glop emotion* that is, it is an emotion made up of many emotions.

When you say you are angry with someone, you usually mean you feel many different feelings at one time for that person. That is why it is a glop emotion.

To complete the emotion anger, you will need to identify all the emotions that make up the anger you have.

Fill out **Worksheet #4 - Anger,** and try to unravel what emotions are making up your anger.

2009 Worksheet #4
2009 Women's Leadership Retreat
Anger

<u>Definition:</u> A strong feeling of displeasure and usually of antagonism from the latin; Angare=to strangle

With whom are you angry?

Why?

What emotion(s) is/are under the anger you feel?

Concept #21
Definition of Abuse

Concept #21
Worksheet #7
2010 Women's Leadership Retreat
Definition of Abuse

- Mistreat: treat badly; "This boss abuses his workers"; "She is always stepping on others to get ahead"

- Pervert: change the inherent purpose or function of something; "Don't abuse the system"; "The director of the factory misused the funds intended for the health care of his workers."

- Maltreatment: cruel or inhumane treatment; "The child showed signs of physical abuse."

- Use of foul or abusive language towards; "The actress abused the policeman who gave her a parking ticket"; "The angry mother shouted at the teacher."

- A rude expression intended to offend or hurt; "When a student made a stupid mistake he spared them no abuse"; "They yelled insults at the visiting team."

- Use wrongly or improperly or excessively: "Her husband often abuses alcohol"; "While she was pregnant, she abused drugs."

- Misuse: improper or excessive use; "alcohol abuse"; "the abuse of public funds"

Worksheet #8
2010 Women's Leadership Retreat
Abuse

Who has abused you at your company?

What did they do?

How did that make you feel?

What did you do about it?

Concept #22

Emotional Abuse –
Silent Voices

Concept #22
Worksheet #9
2010 Women's Leadership Retreat®
Emotional Abuse – Silent Voices

Emotional abuse is a category of abuse no one wants to discuss. It affects the nature of the whole relationship a woman has with a partner. It is not overt like physical abuse so it is harder to detect and treat.

However, it is the most devastating form of abuse because it attacks you at the core of your self-esteem. Some of the victims of emotional abuse don't even know it is going on.

I have seen very successful professional women suffer from emotional abuse at the hands of parents, partners and husbands. Vice-presidents, directors, CEOs - none of these categories are exempt from emotional abuse.

At work, these women command large salaries and bonuses. They may manage millions of dollars in corporate budgets and thousands of people at work, but at home they feel dumb, incompetent and unsuccessful and someone is there to make sure they feel like that all the time.

The very nature of emotional abuse is a slow, chipping away of a women's self-esteem and confidence. If you get told, "you are not good enough" for long enough you start to believe it. The abuser knows this and artfully orchestrates the abuse so you may not even recognize it is going on!

I've seen many forms of emotional abuse. Here are some examples:

1. You are told repeatedly (either in words or by actions) that you are a looser, worthless or incompetent in some way/every way. This is usually around the children or some other home situation. The abuser makes you feel as if you are to blame for any and all problems in the relationship.

2. Your spouse or partner forms a close relationship with your children and/or friends, parents, etc. They use these relationships to put you down and discredit you. You find yourself less and less in relationship with these folks. You treat the abuser with "kid gloves". You "walk on egg shells" and make sure they are never upset. You prepare others to do the same around them or you never allow others to be around them and you.

3. You know they are having an affair, you have evidence that they are. They actually wave it in your face as if to say you are worthless. When you confront them, they deny it and try to make you feel crazy for bringing it up.

4. They never support any ideas, directions, actions or new challenges you want to take on. Sometimes they passively-aggressively go along and then sabotage it. Finally sealing the abuse with comments like "see you said you wanted to do it and now look at what happened!" or "how can you spend so much time away from your family, we need you here."

5. You are completely financially and emotionally responsible for the entire family and the abuser still objects to you spending money or making decisions for the family. They may try to control you through the finances of the family.

If any of these examples ring true for you, you will need to take some action.

First, get yourself into therapy and identify why you accept this kind of abuse and begin to set boundaries for the abuser with your therapist's help. You can set the boundary of them going into therapy as well.

Second, if the abuser continues the abuse or escalates into physical abuse, you must make some important decisions and take action. You may have to leave them. I warn you that without some intervention here it will only get worse. Moreover, if there are children, you are modeling the acceptance of emotional abuse as part of the relationship.

If you find after reading this that you are a part of an emotionally abusive relationship, call a therapist & the police. They will assist you in finding support wherever you are.

Concept #23
Definition of Addiction

Concept #23
Worksheet #10
2010 Women's Leadership Retreat®
Definition of Addiction

An addiction is any process or substance that begins to have control over us in such a way that we feel we must be dishonest with ourselves or others about it.

Addiction is anything we feel we have to lie about. If there is something we are not willing to give up in order to make our lives fuller and more healthy, it probably can be classified as an addiction.

Two forms of addiction:

Substance Addiction, e.g. drug or alcohol or food addiction

Process Addiction, e.g. workaholism

Worksheet #11
2010 Women's Leadership Retreat®
What are you addicted to?

1. What are you addicted to?

2. Can you stop the addiction?
    YES_____

    NO_____

    If so, how?

    If not, why?

3. Are you bad for having this addiction?

4. Are you weak for having this addiction?

5. Are you disgusting for having this addiction?

Concept #24

Definition of Co-dependency

Concept #24
Worksheet #12
2010 Women's Leadership Retreat®
Definition of Co-dependency

Co-dependency is defined by a group of behaviors that emerge because you are or have been a part of an addictive system and/or dysfunctional family patterns. The behaviors that make up a co-dependent are:

1. Dishonesty and Lying: by saying the "nice thing" rather than the truth.

2. Taking Care of Others: they are so giving they give away themselves and become hollow and depressed.

3. Sufferers: They complain a lot, but when you offer help, they refuse to take it.

4. They have Diseases: such as ulcers, high blood pressure, colitis, back pain, and certain types of cancer like breast cancer. Co-dependence is a fatal disease.

5. Frequently in Relationships with Addicts or other Co-Dependents: Stats show co-dependents die younger than addicts do. Co-dependence is a fatal disease.

6. Experts in External Referencing: They spend most of their time understanding the needs of others and picking up subtle cues about others.

7. Rarely Tell You What They Want: They are experts at vagueness, manipulation, rumor and gossip.

8. <u>They use Others as Emotional Surrogates:</u> Others get angry, sad, hurt for them and then fight their battles for them.

Co-dependency is a more subtle and socially acceptable disease then addiction. Culturally, they look like loving, giving people. They are often described as "the nicest person I know". Underneath this exterior they are angry, depressed, and extremely controlling and manipulative.

Worksheet #13
2010 Women's Leadership Retreat®
Co-Dependency Worksheet

1. Are you co-dependent?
   YES _____
   NO _____

   If yes, why?

   If no, why?

2. Are you an emotional surrogate for someone?
   YES _____
   NO _____

   If yes, for whom? List Them:
   _____
   _____

3. Are you a martyr?
   YES _____
   NO _____

   If so, about what?

4. Are you a benefactor?
   YES _____
   NO _____

   If so, for whom and why?

5. Who gets to be irresponsible because you are co-dependent?

Concept #25
Neurotic/Psychotic Chart

Concept # 25

Worksheet #14

2011 Women's Leadership Retreat ®

Neurotic/ Psychotic Chart

Neurotics	Psychotics
They are in this world and in reality.	They are not in this world and they are *not* in reality.
Responding to the world with a series of protective behaviors or safety mechanisms. Responses are fear based.	They are in their psychosis instead of the world. They respond to keep psychosis in place. They live in the delusion(s) they build to be safe. They believe their delusion *is* reality.
Situationally Neurotic People can become Neurotic after great loss or injury, especially if tendencies for neurosis are already there.	**Psychotic Break** Where a seemingly normal person "breaks down" and becomes delusional.

Worksheet # 15
2011 Women's Leadership Retreat®
Behaviors to Assess

Using Neurotic / Psychotic Chart (Worksheet #5), are the behaviors listed below Psychotic or Neurotic?

1. Held hostage – extortion. If you don't do this, I'll do that or if you do this, I'll do that.

2. Bullying/Intimidating/Coercing

3. Demanding to be the center of attention, always making themselves the issue.

4. Gossiping to manipulate a situation; work or personal.

5. Controlling – must know what will happen next – must be in control at all times, must go by their own rules or won't do anything.

6. Use work to punish employees/peers/clients/customers.

7. Discrediting/Character Assassination.

8. Throwing data and terminology around all the time, rather than speaking clearly.

Concept #26
Mental Illnesses Prevalent in Corporations

Concept #26
Worksheet # 16
2011 Women's Leadership Retreat®
Mental Illnesses Prevalent in Corporations

These are the Mental Illnesses we and others have seen in Corporations.

Anxiety Disorders:
Obsessive Compulsive Personality Disorder (OCD)
Post Traumatic Stress Disorder (PTSD)
Panic Disorder
Social Phobia
Specific Phobias
Generalized Anxiety Disorder

Other Disorders:
Bipolar Disorder (Manic / Depression)
Clinical Depression
Narcissistic Personality Disorder
Schizophrenia
Paranoia/ Paranoid Disorder
Sociopath
Psychopath
Addiction

Anxiety Disorders:
Obsessive Compulsive Personality Disorder (OCPD)
Pre-occupation w/orderliness, perfectionism & control

NIMH Descriptions;
Obsessive Compulsive Disorder (OCD)
Persistent, upsetting thoughts (obsessions) and use rituals (compulsions) to control anxiety these thoughts produce. The rituals usually end up controlling them (Monk)

Post Traumatic Stress Disorder (PTSD)
Re-experiencing of an extremely traumatic event that involved physical harm or the threat of physical harm, increased arousal (hyper –vigilance), avoidance of stimuli. (war-veterans but also abuse victims and folks in NY after 9-11)

Panic Disorder
Sudden attacks of terror accompanied by heart pounding, sweatiness, weakness, faintness or dizziness. They produce a fear of impending doom or fear of loss of control

Social Phobia also called Social Anxiety Disorder
Person becomes overwhelmingly anxious and excessively self-conscious in every day social situations. Intense persistent and chronic fear of being watched and judged by others and of doing things that will embarrass them.

Specific Phobias
An intense irrational fear of something that poses little or no threat, fears of specific things or situations: Agoraphobia, Xenophobia, and claustrophobia

Generalized Anxiety Disorder (GAD)
Exaggerated worry and tension, even though there is little or nothing to provoke it.

Other Disorders Prevalent in Companies:
(Addictions see 2010)
Bipolar Disorder (Manic / Depression)

Cycling of mania & depression. In Depression Cycle = appetite changes, weight loss or gain, sleep disorders, loss of interest (in men depression manifests as anger sometimes) feelings of worthlessness and guilt.

In Mania Cycle = Increased activity, gambling, sexual activity, hyper activity, lack of sleep a feeling of accomplishing much and being very creative

Clinical Depression

Changes in Appetite, weight, sleep, psychomotor activity (In men Anger), difficulty thinking, feelings of worthlessness and guilt.

Narcissistic Personality Disorder

Pervasive pattern of grandiosity & self importance. Need for admiration as well as lack of empathy. They believe they are superior special and unique. Expect others to recognize this and react to them accordingly. Really covers and extremely low or non-existing self-image and low self-confidence.

Schizophrenia

Delusions (hearing voices), hallucinations (seeing things that aren't there), disorganized speech (each sentence makes sense but not put together with the next sentence), Catatonia, flat or no affect, lack of fluency and focus.

Paranoia/ Paranoid Disorder

Pattern of distrust and suspicion, others are attacking you and after you (may have it's basis in fact)

Sociopath

In reality but no internalized values. No discerning right or wrong

Psychopath

Psyhotic and no internalized values. No right or wrong

Personality Disorders

An enduring pattern of behavior that deviates markedly from expectations of the individual's culture. The behavior is pervasive and inflexible. Jeffrey Dahmer

Worksheet # 17
Normal to Psychotic Chart

Normal   Neurotic   Psychotic

>>>

In times of great stress people take a step to the right!

If you have been abused:

Abuse in Your History =
High Control Needs =
A False Sense of Comfort (Security)

To raise healthy kids = Model what being healthy looks like

How to Contact Us

Susan Van Vleet Consultants, Inc ® (SVVCI®) works with a diverse group of companies and organizations across the world.

SVVCI® can design programs for your company or organization that meet your immediate and long-term needs.

You can find us through our websites, as well as through LinkedIn and FaceBook.

You can also contact us directly:

Susan Van Vleet Consultants, Inc.
31416 Agoura Rd. Ste 255
Westlake Village, CA. 91361
Phone 303.660.5206
Email svvconsult@svanvleetconsult.com

Websites:

Svanvleetconsult.com and womenmovingforward.com

Our Distributors
Lorrie Teitze
Interface Consulting
lbtietze@interfaceconsultingonline.com

Robin Elston
Elston Consulting, LLC
relston@bright.net

Kate Gruninger Johnson
Gracecamp Consulting
Kate@gracecamp.com